Fruitful Colors:
A Harvest of Fruits and Vegetables Coloring Book

by diedude

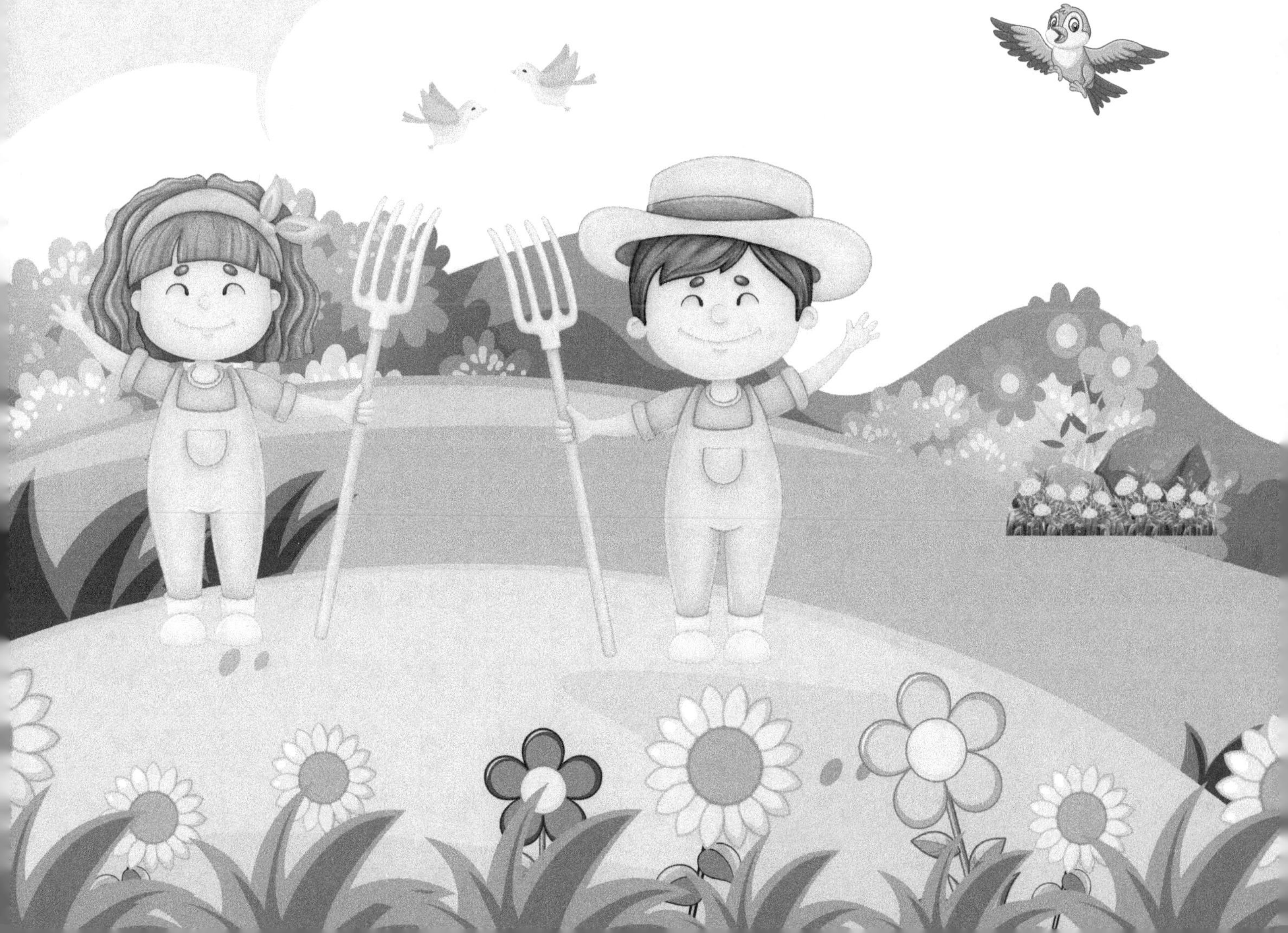

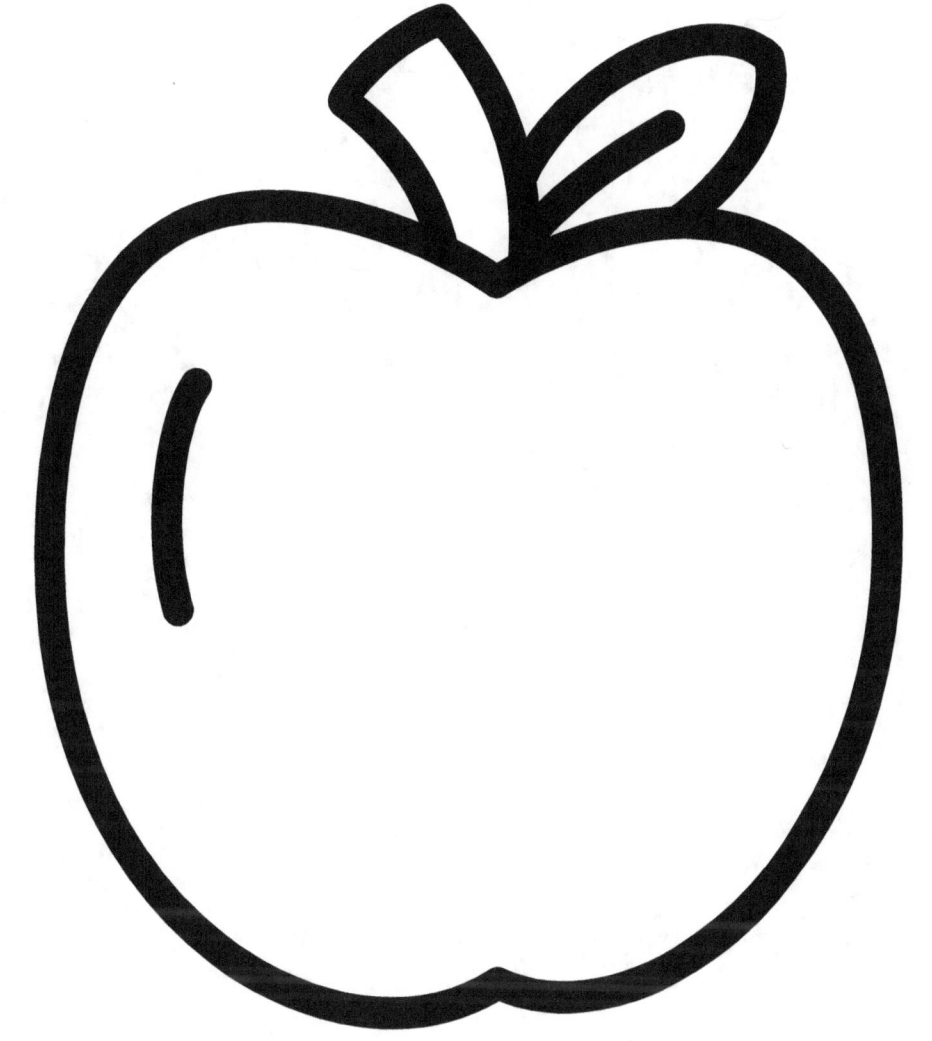

APPLE

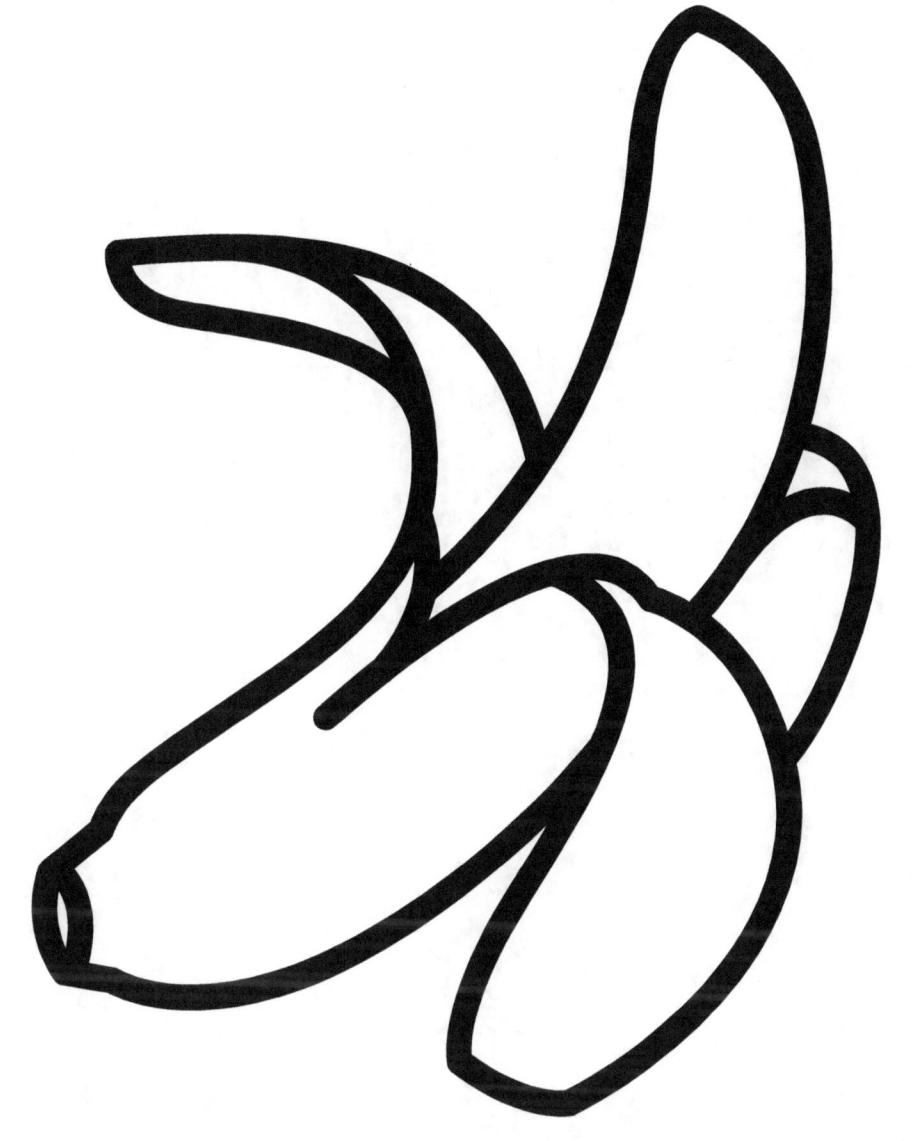

BANANA

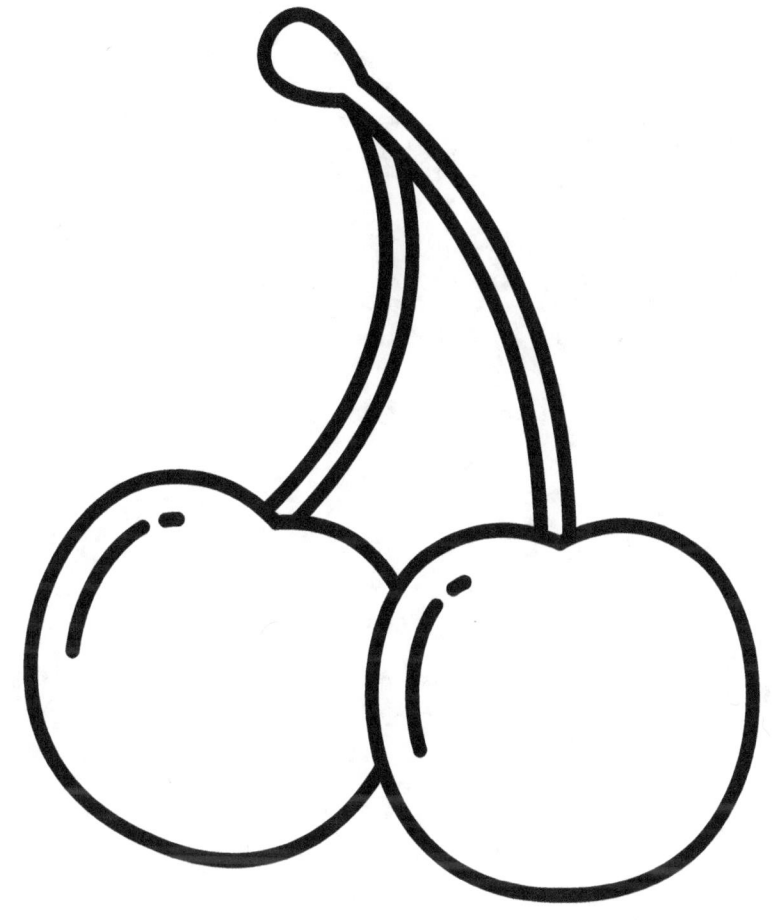

CHERRY

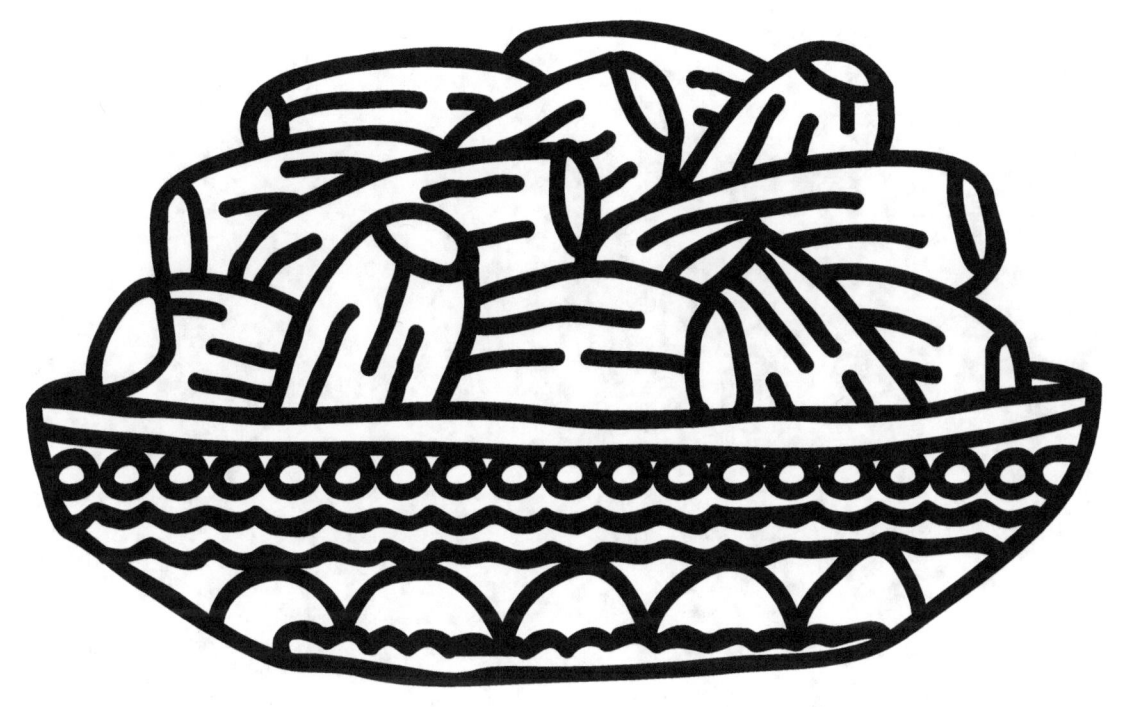

DATES

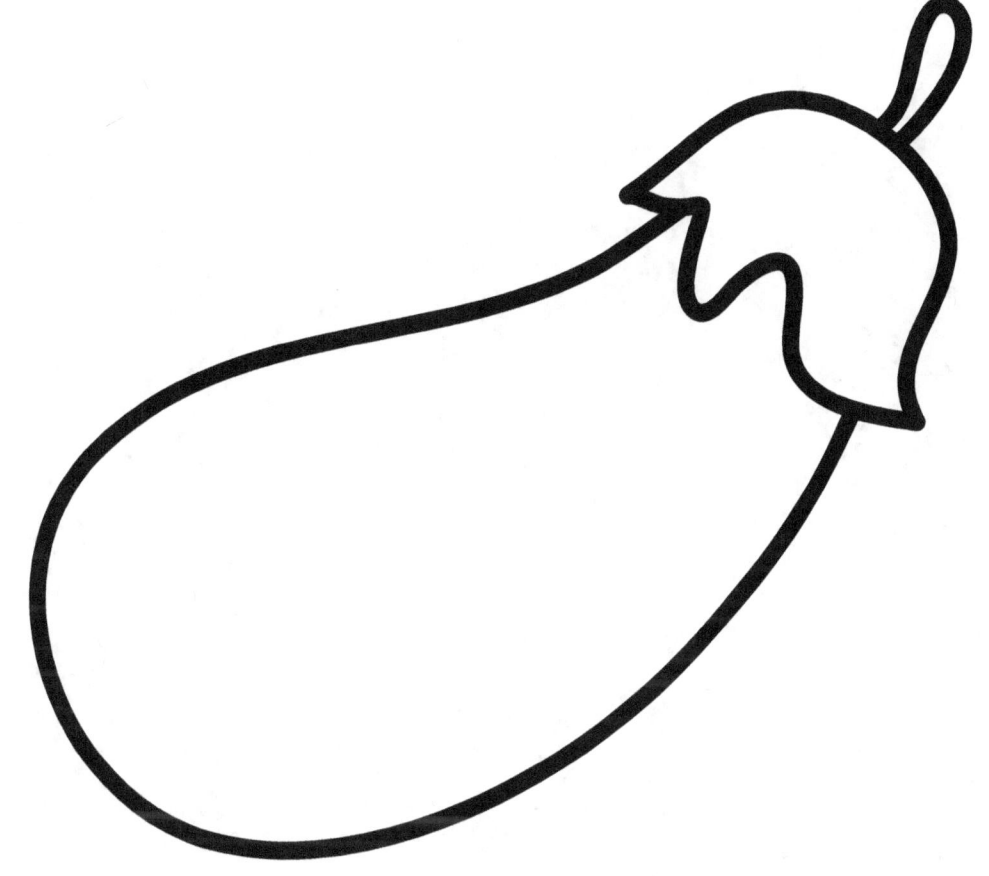

EGGPLANT

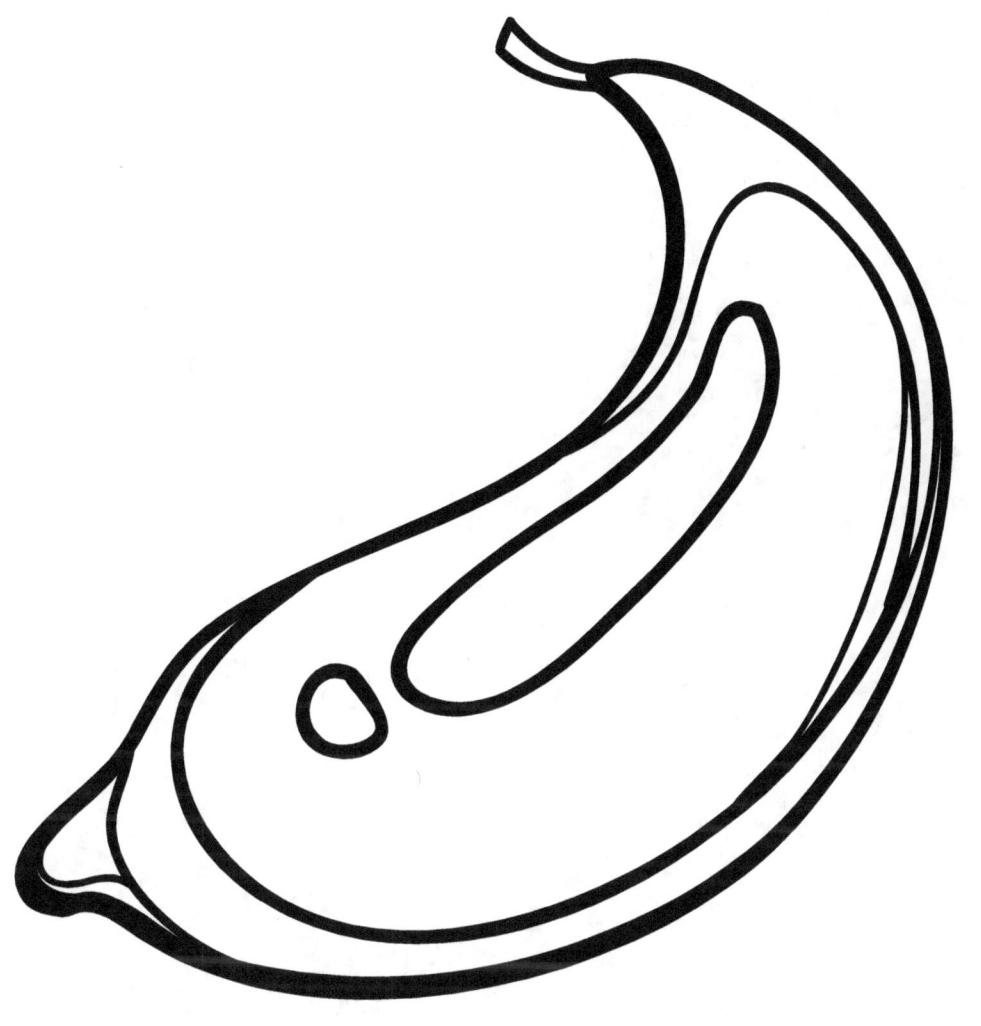

FINGER LIME

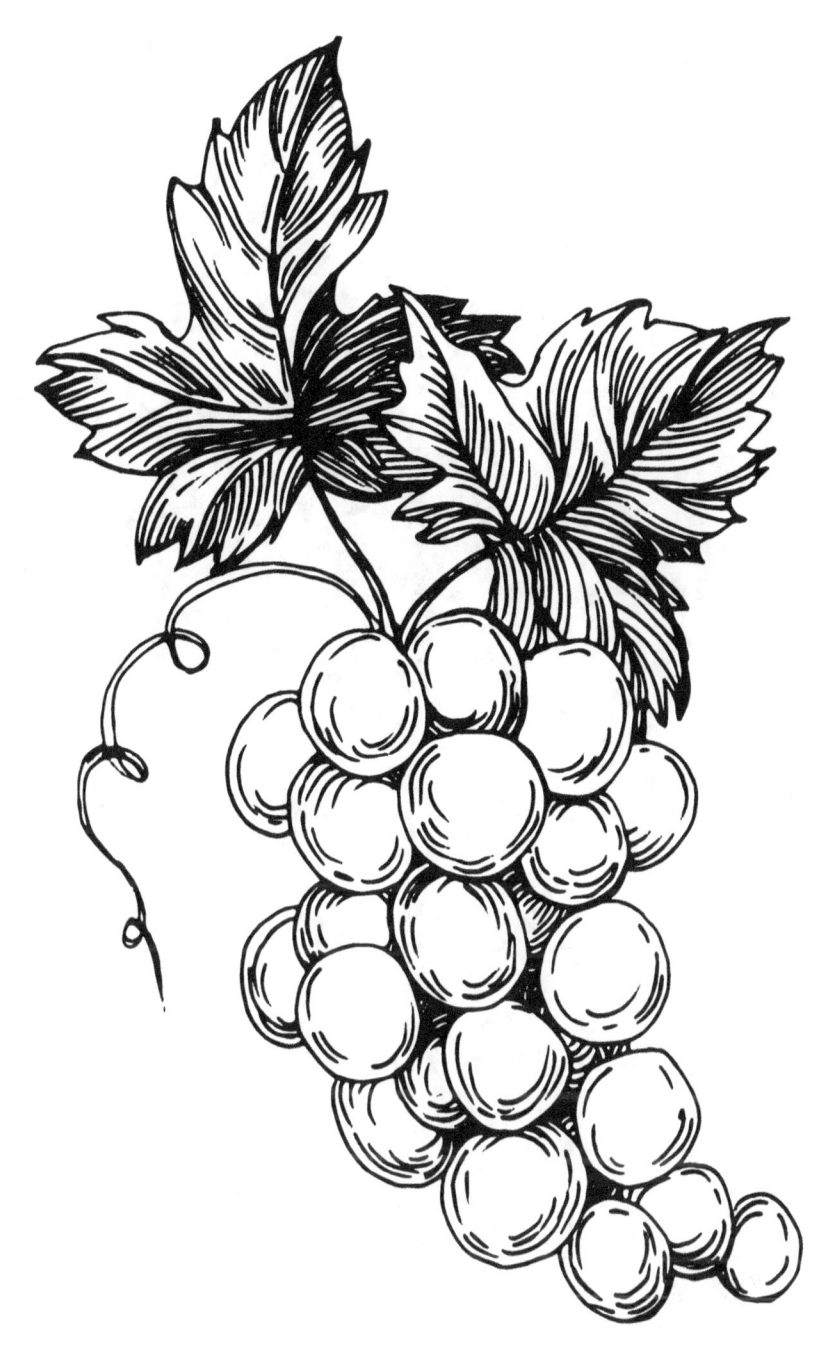

GRAPES

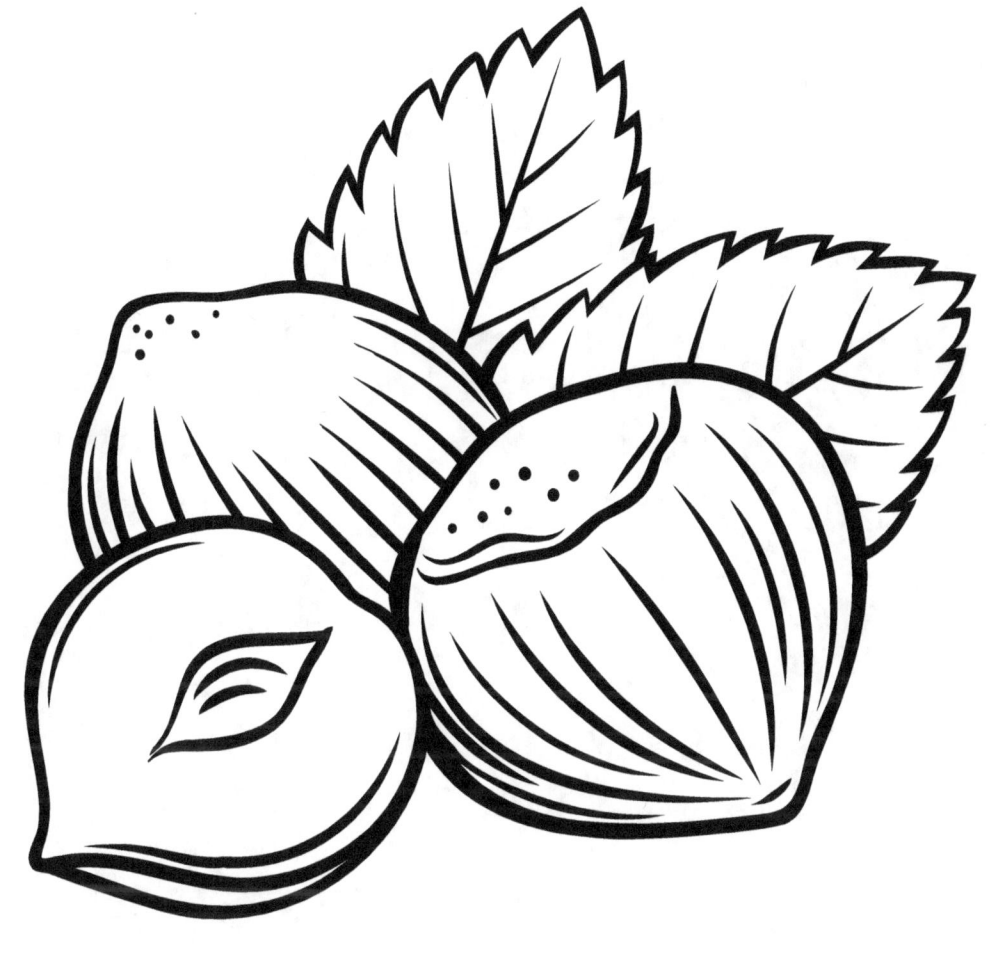

HAZELNUT

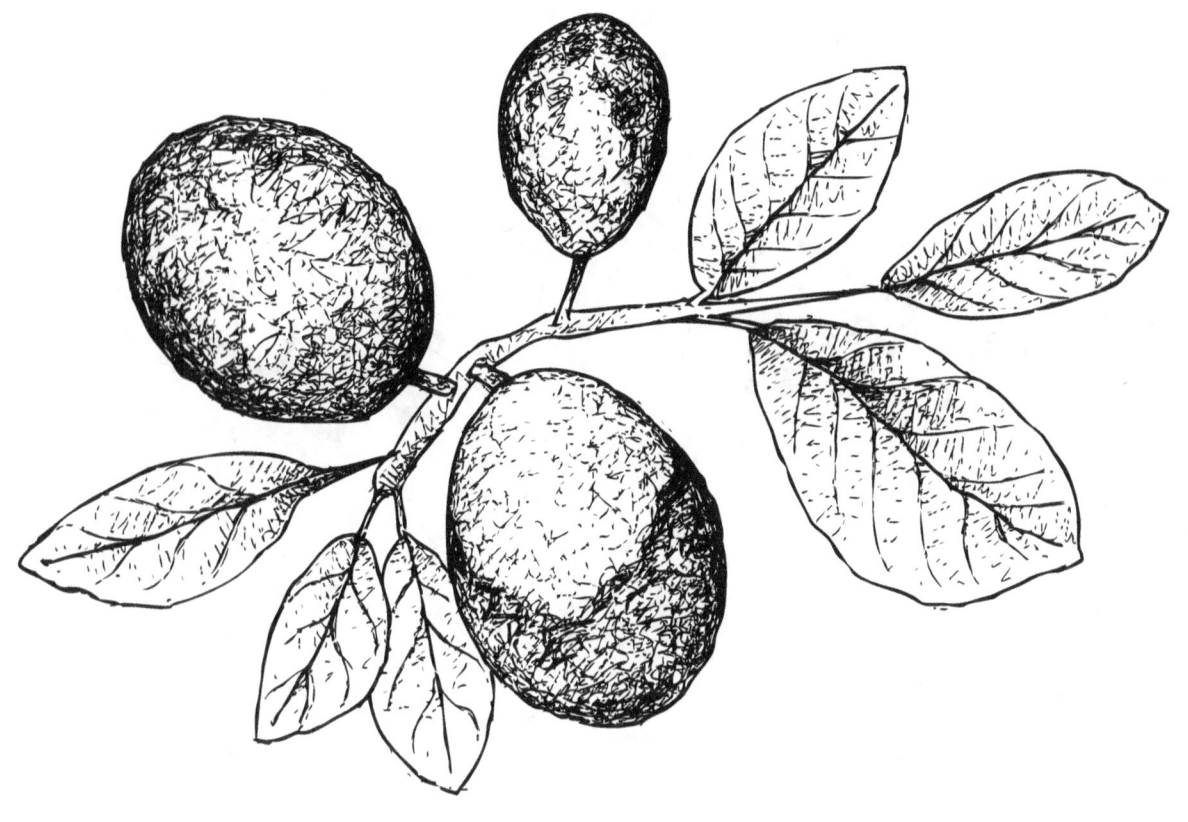

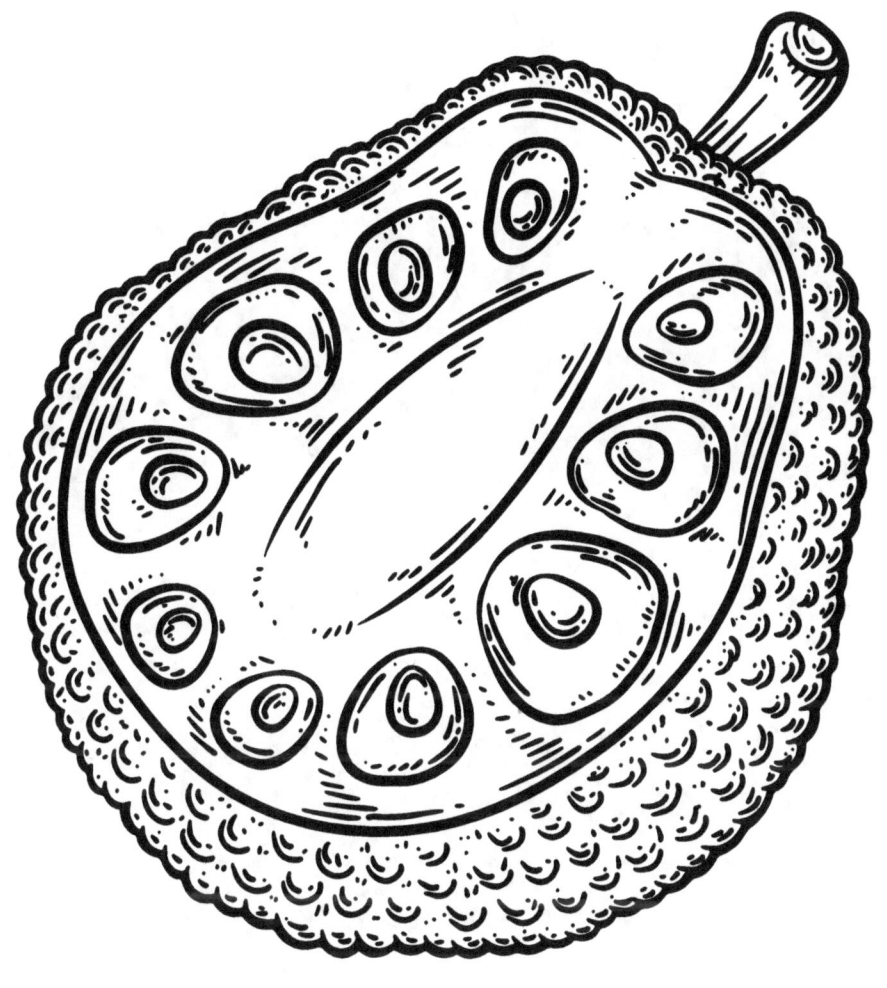

JACKFRUIT

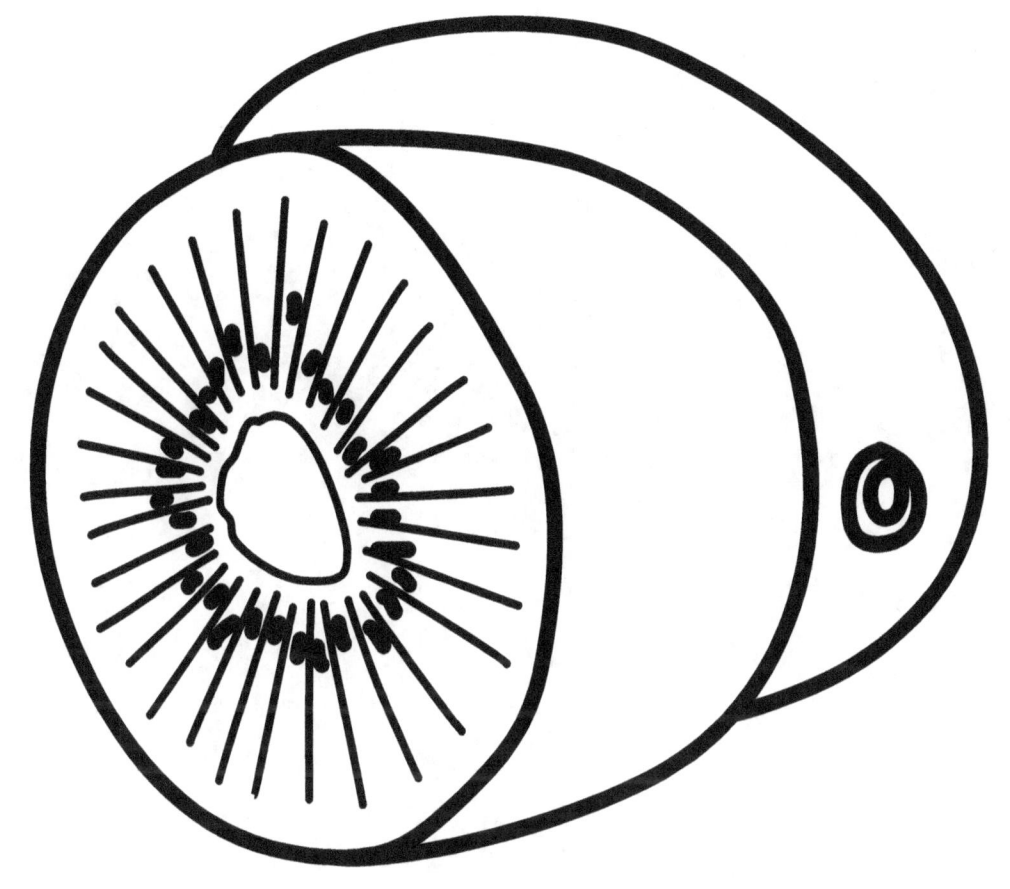

kiwi

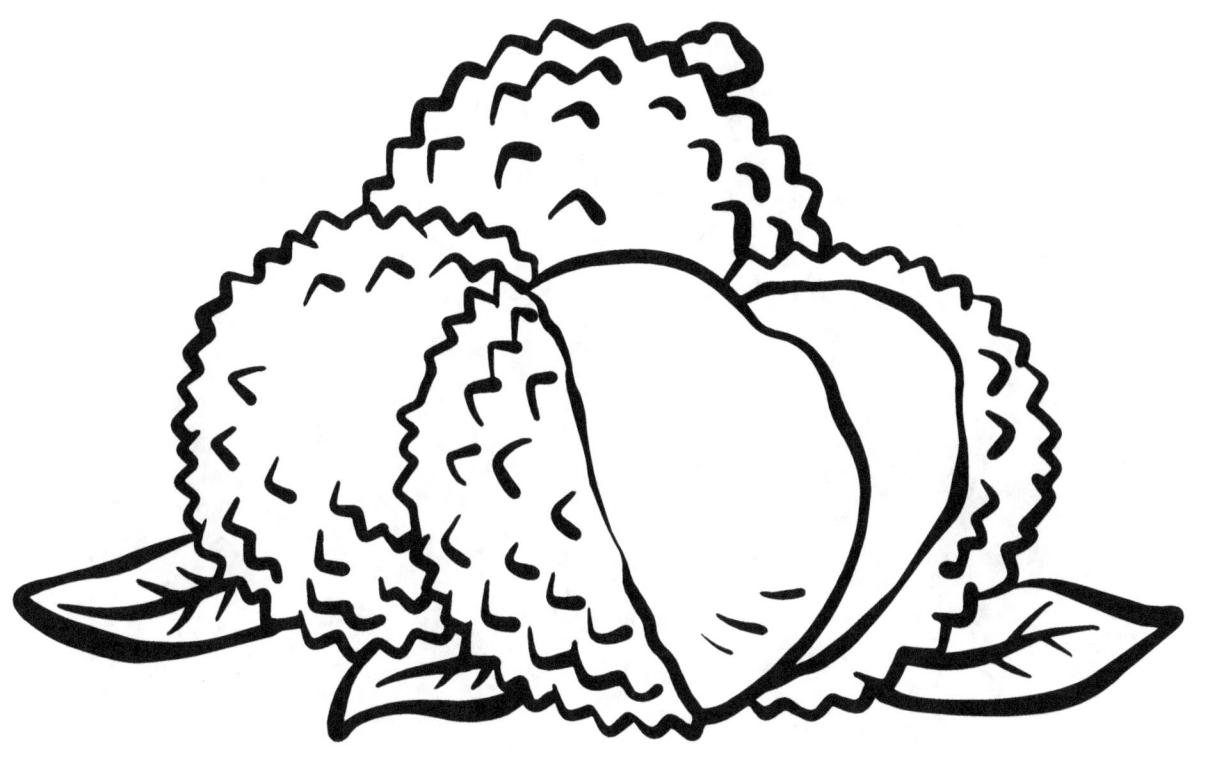

LYCHEE

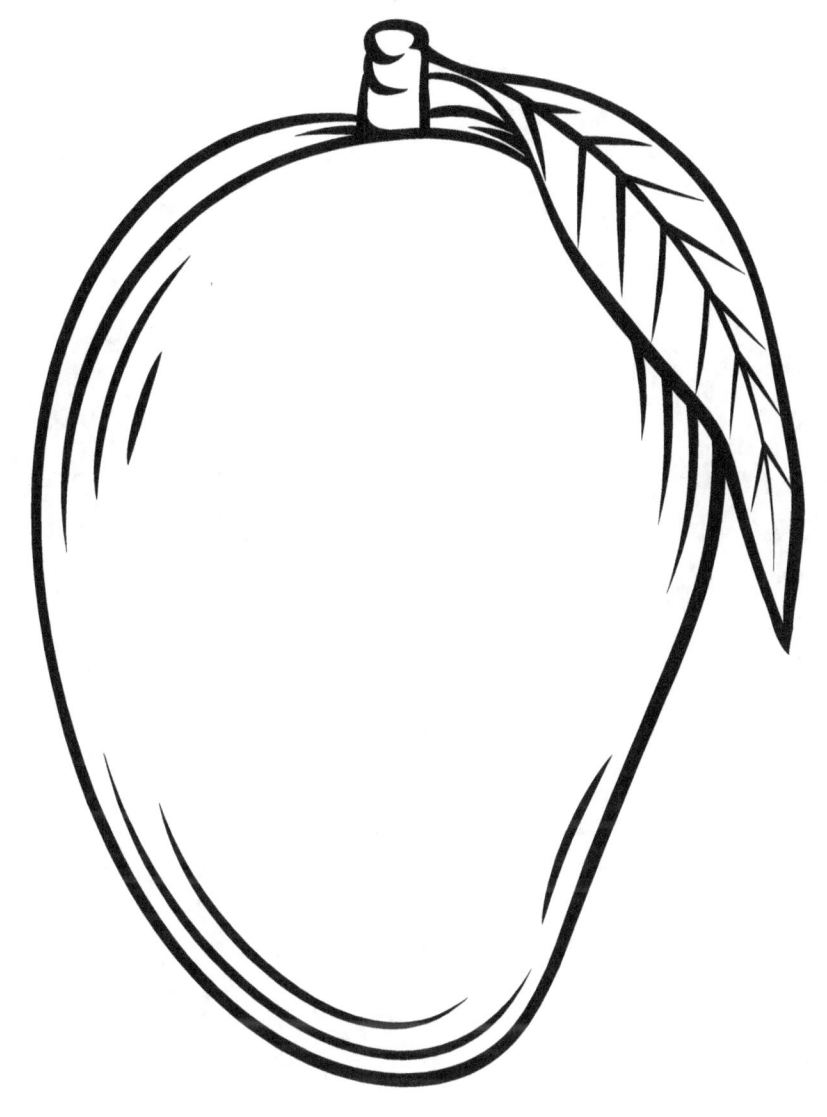

MANGO

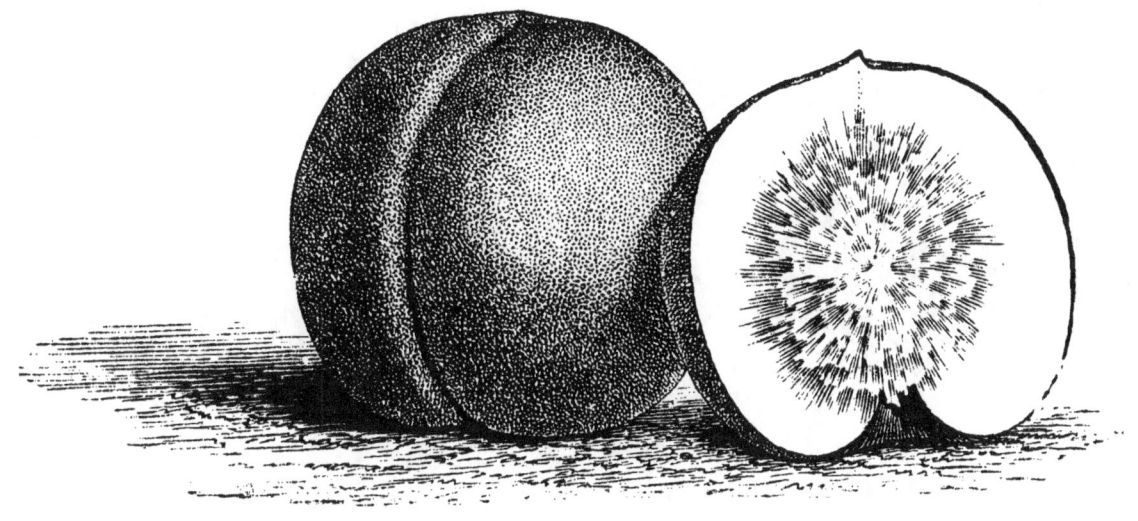

NECTARINES

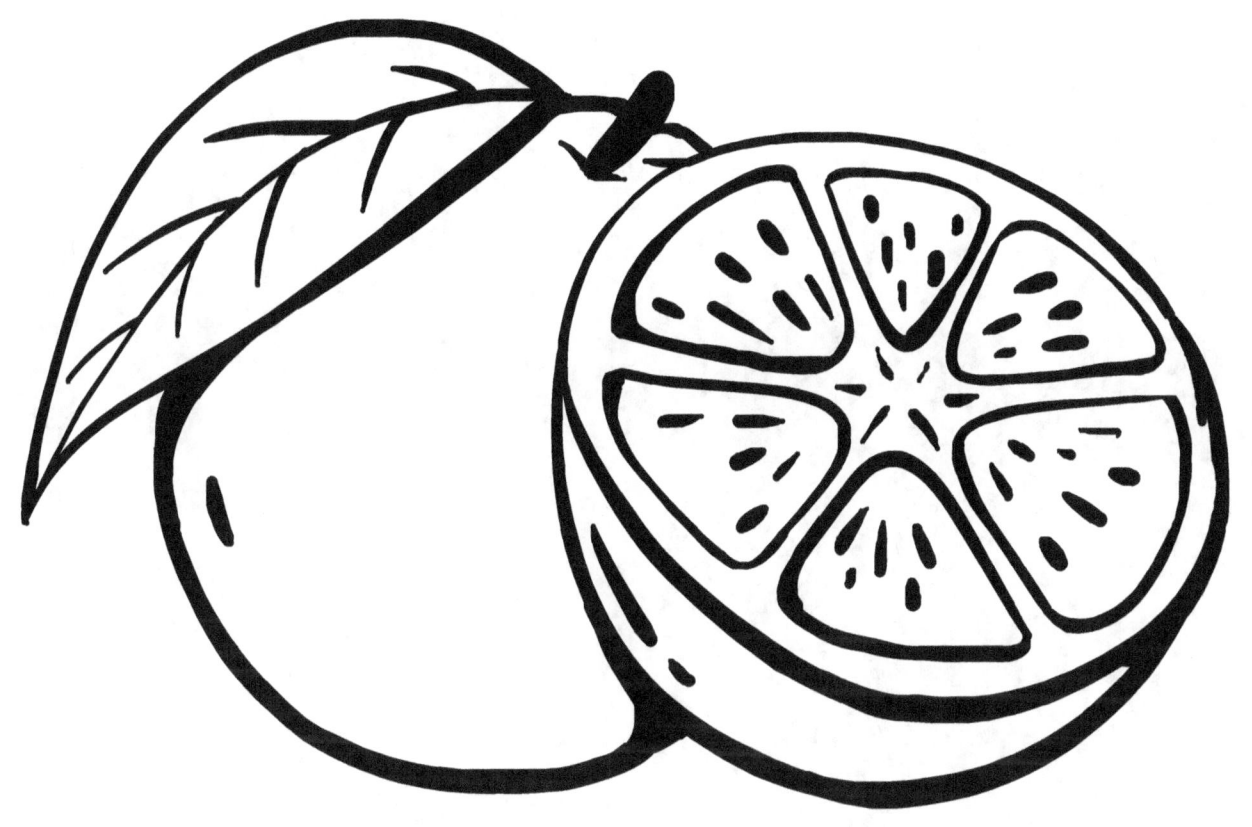

ORANGE

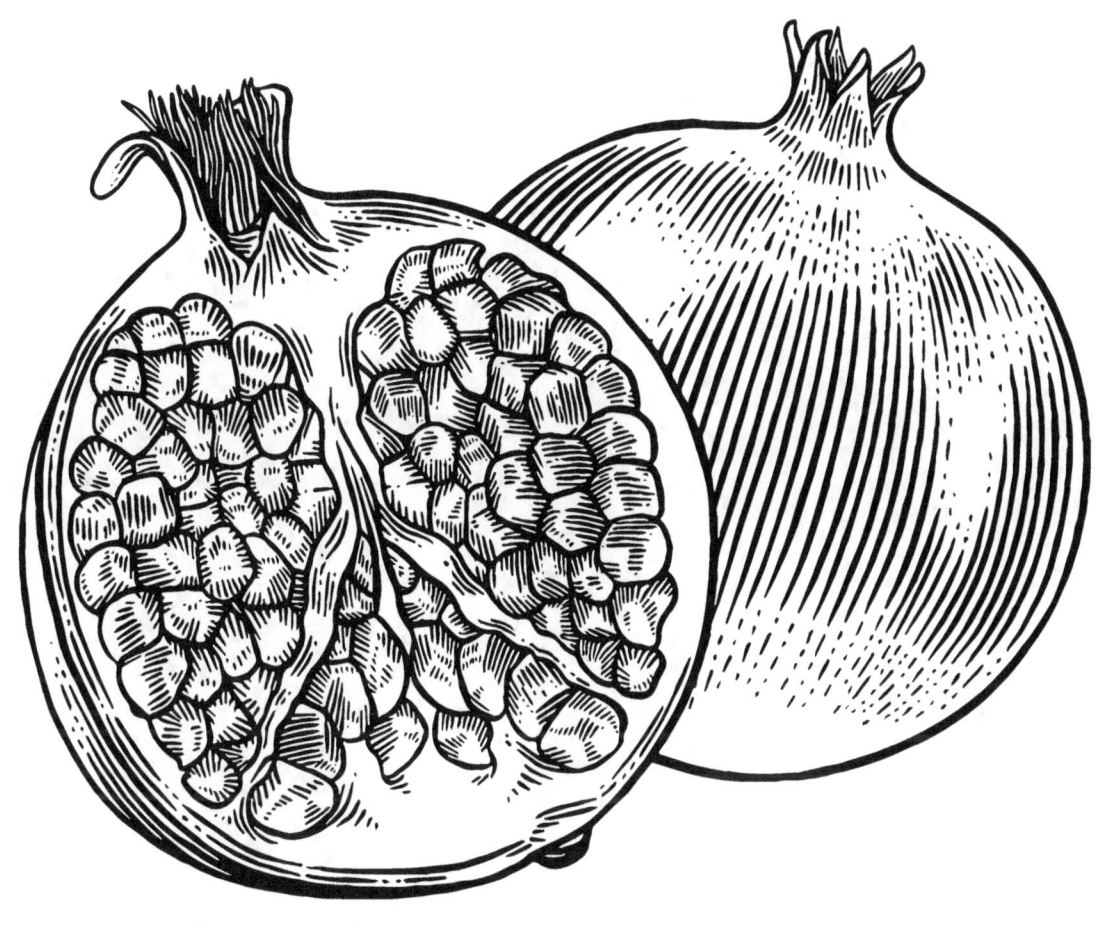

POMEGRANATE

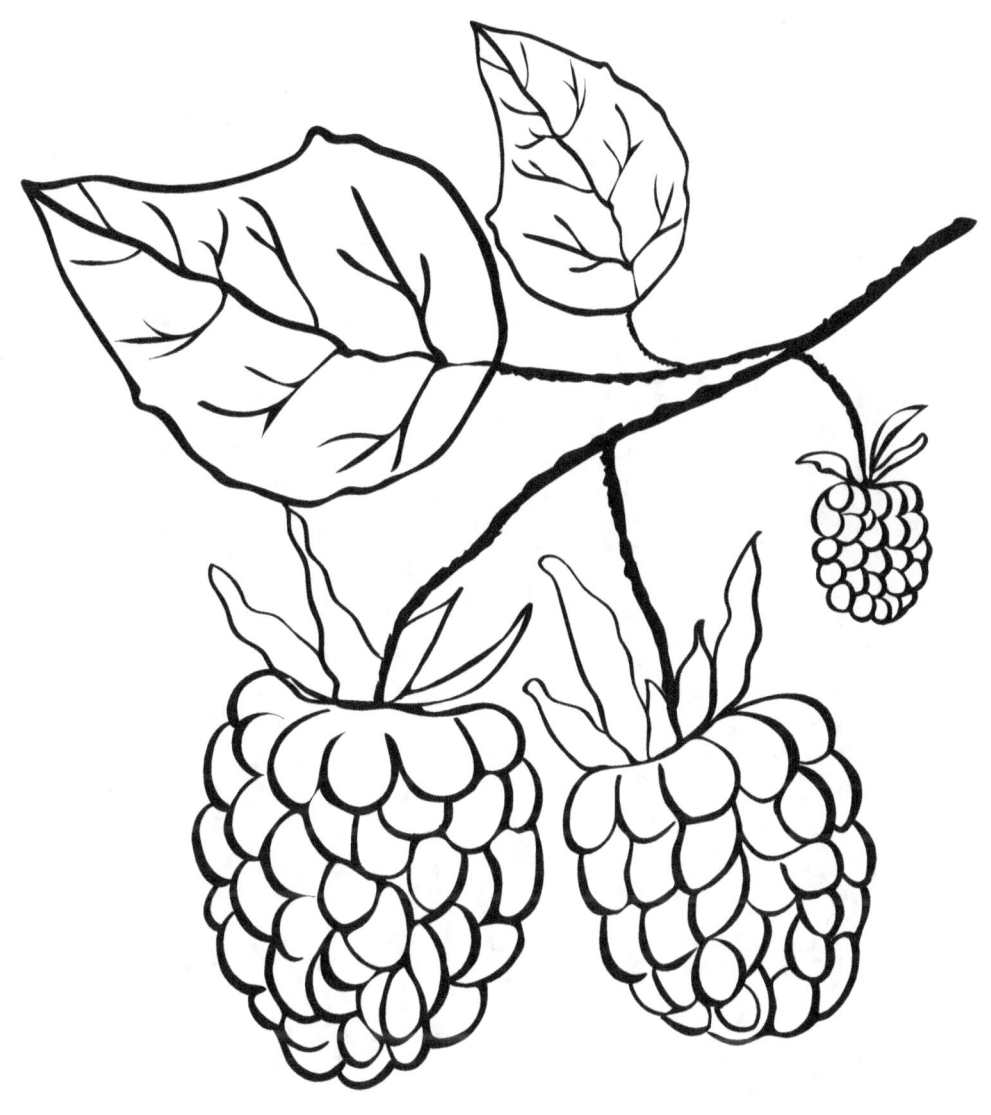

STRAWBERRY

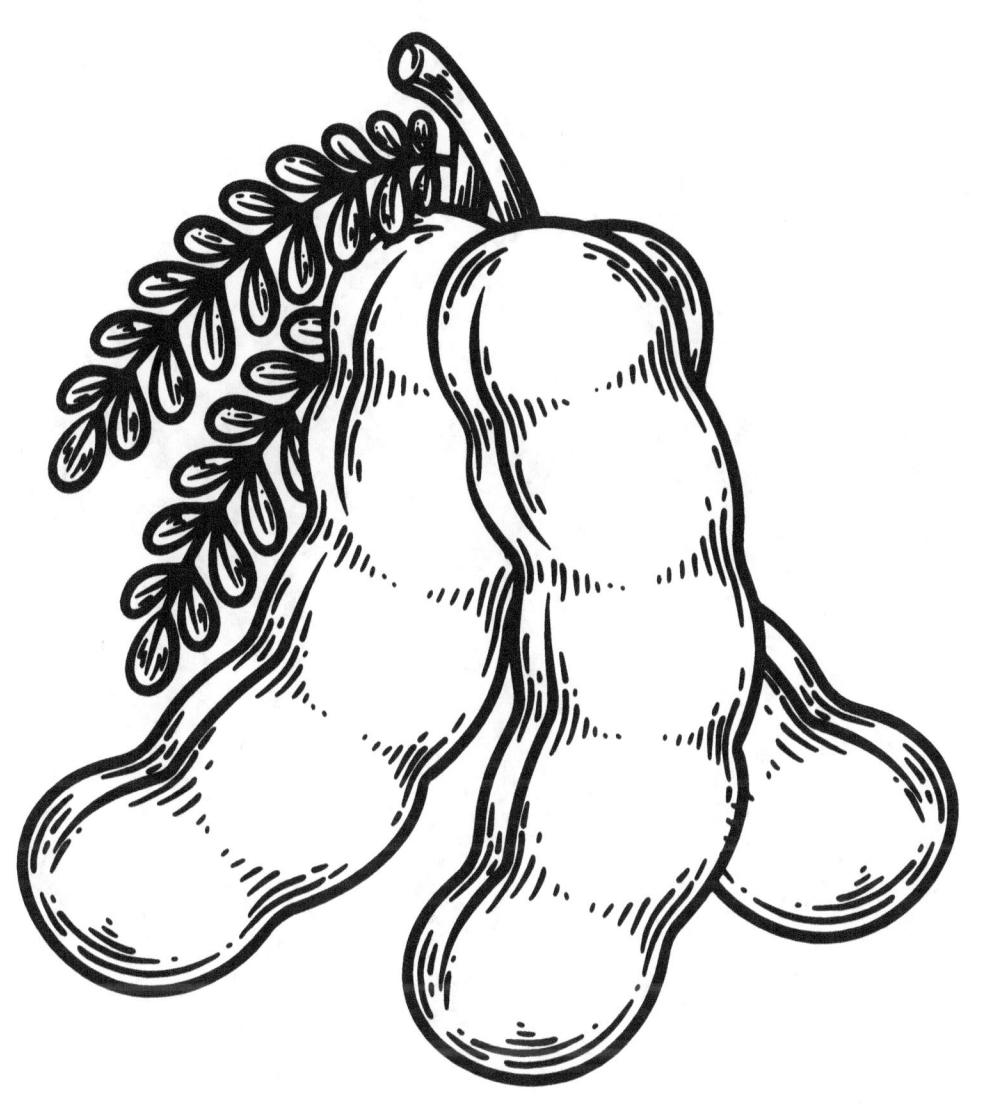

TAMARIND

www.ingramcontent.com/pod-product-compliance
Lightning Source LLC
Chambersburg PA
CBHW082223220526
45470CB00010B/3285